MARILYN MONROE

A POSTCARD BOOK

John Marriott

RUNNING PRESS
PHILADELPHIA, PENNSYLVANIA

Postcard Book is a trademark of Running Press Book Publishers.

9 8 7 6 5 4 3 2 1
The digit on the right indicates the number of this printing.

ISBN 0-89471-898-3
Front and back cover photograph
Title page photograph

Printed and bound in Singapore

This book may be ordered by mail from the Publisher. Please add $2.50 for postage and handling. *But try your bookstore first!* Running Press Book Publishers, 125 South Twenty-second Street, Philadelphia, Pennsylvania 19103.

Introduction

The most renowned of screen goddesses, Marilyn Monroe's electric appeal has flourished for more than three decades. She exuded a charismatic combination of girlish innocence and sultry sophistication that made her bigger than any of the roles she played.

Marilyn's glamour was tempered with an edge of innocence. Her vulnerability was genuine and deeply-felt, the result of a troubled childhood with a mentally ill mother and no father.

Born Norma Jean Baker, Marilyn Monroe was discovered by an Army photographer while working as a paint sprayer in a defense plant. Her photos boosted the morale of wartime troops and led to a postwar modeling career, which was Marilyn's entree to Hollywood.

Her success wasn't instantaneous. She paid her dues as a pinup girl, a member of the chorus, the footage left on the cutting-room floor, and the rest of Hollywood's legendary indignities. But slowly, people began to take notice.

And then, like Venus rising from the sea, America's Goddess ascended. Now came the fabulous film deals. Now the high-profile marriages. Now the glamour, the adoration of millions. Then came the pressures, the demands, the personal problems of a public figure.

America never fully recovered from the death of Marilyn Monroe. She holds an unique place in our culture and in our hearts. She is missed.

This coolly coquetish pinup highlights Marilyn's casual
magnetism.

PHOTOGRAPH: REX FEATURES/STILLS

Marilyn's girlish glee helped launch her into a legendary
career.

PHOTOGRAPH: CAMERA PRESS

Marilyn's wonderful vitality brightening Jones Beach,
New York, 1950.

PHOTOGRAPH: REX FEATURES

Star trappings and a confident attitude won Marilyn the
adoration of millions.

PHOTOGRAPH: REX FEATURES/STILLS

Marilyn's comic timing proved a fitting match for the
talents of Tony Curtis and Jack Lemmon in Billy
Wilder's milestone *Some Like It Hot* (1959).

PHOTOGRAPH: THE KOBAL COLLECTION

Marilyn loved the outdoors, where she could take a
break from reporters and the throngs of fans. This 1955
photo shows how she could look glamorous in any
setting.

PHOTOGRAPH: CAMERA PRESS/M. GREENE

The chic, sophisticated Marilyn Monroe in 1962.

PHOTOGRAPH: CAMERA PRESS/L. SCHILLER

After a shaky start in films, Marilyn became a
formidable screen presence.

PHOTOGRAPH: THE KOBAL COLLECTION

Marilyn received her first taste of star treatment when
she signed with 20th Century Fox in 1944. At Fox she
was given acting, singing, and dancing lessons, plugs in
gossip columns, and dates with celebrities.

PHOTOGRAPH: L.F.I.

Friend and photographer Andre de Dienes took this
picture of Norma Jean Dougherty during a trip through
California in 1945.

PHOTOGRAPH: CAMERA PRESS/ANDRE DE DIENES

At the height of her career, Marilyn was photographed
by Philippe Halsman.

PHOTOGRAPH: CAMERA PRESS/P. HALSMAN

The sultry Marilyn Monroe early in her career.

PHOTOGRAPH: L.F.I.

Marilyn as a saloon singer with a gold claim in *River of No Return* (1955).

PHOTOGRAPH: REX FEATURES

Although the public adored her, Marilyn wasn't the
easiest actress to direct. Director George Cukor
suspended her from *Something's Got to Give* because of
her lateness. The film was never completed.

PHOTOGRAPH: REX FEATURES/STILLS

Early in her career and between movie contracts,
Marilyn posed for several publicity pictures.

PHOTOGRAPH: REX FEATURES/STILLS

Marilyn successfully shucked her innocent, little girl
image by posing for photographs such as this one.

PHOTOGRAPH: CAMERA PRESS/DOUGLAS KIRKLAND

"A POSTCARD BOOK™"
© 1990 BY RUNNING PRESS BOOK PUBLISHERS

The key to Marilyn's appeal was her paradoxical
combination of feline sensuality and playful innocence.

PHOTOGRAPH: CAMERA PRESS

A fresh-faced Norma Jean Dougherty begins her climb
to superstardom in 1954.

PHOTOGRAPH: CAMERA PRESS/ANDRE DE DIENES

Perhaps the most famous scene in screen history, this shot from *The Seven Year Itch* (1955) has become a part of America's collective consciousness. With Marilyn is her co-star, Tom Ewell.

PHOTOGRAPH: REX FEATURES

In *Niagara* (1953), Marilyn played a sinister woman who plots to murder her new husband.

PHOTOGRAPH: THE KOBAL COLLECTION

In *The Misfits* (1960), Marilyn portrayed a melancholy divorcee. The screenplay was written by her husband, Arthur Miller, and directed by John Huston. It was Marilyn's last film.

PHOTOGRAPH: REX FEATURES/FOTOS INTERNATIONAL

The spotlight is on Marilyn Monroe as Miss Vicky
Parker in *There's No Business Like Show Business* (1954).
This Fox musical featured Irving Berlin songs and a
very sexy Marilyn.

PHOTOGRAPH: REX FEATURES

Tired of being typecast as a dumb blonde, Marilyn
founded Marilyn Monroe Productions and studied
acting with Lee Strasberg.

PHOTOGRAPH: THE KOBAL COLLECTION

Marilyn Monroe was just another model in this early,
self-conscious publicity still.

PHOTOGRAPH: REX FEATURES

Marilyn in the 20th Century Fox film *Let's Make Love*
(1961), a musical comedy directed by George Cukor and
co-starring Yves Montand and Frankie Vaughan.

PHOTOGRAPH: THE KOBAL COLLECTION

Taking a break from filming *Bus Stop* (1956), Marilyn
poses for a publicity picture. She played a saloon singer
pursued by an amorous cowboy.

PHOTOGRAPH: CAMERA PRESS/M. GREENE

Marilyn's disarming smile won many fans. No matter
how high her star ascended, she always seemed to have
a sense of the girl next door.

PHOTOGRAPH: REX FEATURES/SIPA

The Hitchcock–style melodrama *Niagara* (1953) was
Marilyn Monroe's first real break in films.

Carefree and exuberant, Marilyn leaps along the beach
at Amangansett, Long Island, where she and Arthur
Miller had a summer house in 1958.

PHOTOGRAPH: CAMERA PRESS/SAM SHAW

Marilyn Monroe's kisses still linger.

PHOTOGRAPH: REX FEATURES